IDEAS FOR USING
BIG BOOKS

KS1

P1 to 3

UNIVERSITY COLLEGE C_____ _____RIES

AUTHOR:

STEPHENSON

TITLE:

IDEAS

DATE: 10-2000

O CR 823.07

TES

D1391044

AUTHOR
Chris Stephenson

DESIGNER
Rachael Hammond

EDITOR
Jean Coppendale

ILLUSTRATIONS
Ann Kronheimer

ASSISTANT EDITOR
Kate Pearce

COVER ARTWORK
Ian Murray

SERIES DESIGNER
Anna Oliwa

Text © 2000 Chris Stephenson
© 2000 Scholastic Ltd

Designed using Adobe Pagemaker
Published by Scholastic Ltd, Villiers House, Clarendon
Avenue, Leamington Spa, Warwickshire CV32 5PR

1234567890   0123456789

British Library Cataloguing-in-Publication Data
A catalogue record for this book is available from the
British Library.

ISBN 0-439-01741-6

The right of Chris Stephenson to be identified as the
author of this work has been asserted by her in
accordance with the Copyright, Designs and Patents
Act 1988.

All rights reserved. This book is sold subject to the
condition that it shall not, by way of trade or otherwise,
be lent, hired out or otherwise circulated without the
publisher's prior consent in any form of binding or cover
other than that in which it is published and without a
similar condition, including this condition, being imposed
upon the subsequent purchaser.

No part of this publication may be reproduced, stored
in a retrieval system, or transmitted, in any form or by
any means, electronic, mechanical, photocopying,
recording or otherwise, without the prior permission
of the publisher. This book remains copyright, although
permission is granted to copy those pages marked
'Photocopiables' for classroom distribution and use
only in the school which has purchased the book and
in accordance with the CLA licensing agreement.
Photocopying permission is given only for purchasers
and not for borrowers of books from any lending
service.

Contents

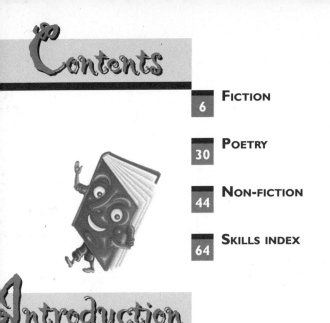

Introduction

CHOOSING BIG BOOKS

More and more classroom Big Books have become available since the introduction of the National Literacy Strategy. The training videos produced by the NLS for the Literacy Hour presented shared reading sessions that focused on Big Books as a model of good teaching practice, and publishers have been quick to respond.

FICTION AND POETRY

With so many Big Book titles on the market, it is important to choose with care which titles to use. The quality of Big Book fiction is, on the whole, very good. Many excellent picture books for young children are now available in Big Book formats, including old favourites such as *The Very Hungry Caterpillar* by Eric Carle (published by Longman), *Dogger* by Shirley Hughes (Red Fox) and *Each Peach, Pear, Plum* by Janet and Allan Ahlberg (Viking), as well as more recent titles such as *The Hunter* by Paul Geraghty (Red Fox) and *Suddenly!* by Colin McNaughton (Collins). Buying titles such as these gives you the option of using them alongside the original small-format version; a great advantage for individual children, and also if you need to carry the book home for lesson preparation! Popular reading schemes such as *Story Chest* (Kingscourt Publications) have been offering Big Book versions of titles in their group reading sets for some time. Above all, choose stories that you enjoy reading yourself, that are rich in teaching possibilities, and presented in a format large enough for a whole class to see the words and appreciate the detail of the illustrations.

Big Book poetry anthologies vary in quality and may not always be available in small format. *Laughing Giraffes* (Kingscourt Publications) and *Our Favourite Rhymes* (Longman) are referred to in the activities (see pages 32–34). Another collection well

worth buying is *If You Should Meet a Crocodile* (published by Macmillan), a lively mix of classic and modern poems about wild animals that older infants will relish, and many of which are fun to learn by heart. Other poetry titles specifically referred to in the activities are simple rhyming narratives which might also be classified as stories. In this category, *Pass the Jam, Jim* by Kaye Umansky (Red Fox) deserves mention as a wonderful exercise in alliteration and word play.

NON-FICTION

The non-fiction Big Books published so far vary in quality; the content is very thin and ill thought-through in some cases. The books that set out to model the structure and research devices of more adult reference texts (with mini contents, an index and glossary) tend to be the least informative as far as hard facts are concerned. They may be useful in teaching alphabetical order and very simple research skills, but will not answer many of the questions raised by an inquiring infant. Books that approach non-fiction topics in a less formal way such *as A Seed in Need* by Sam Godwin (published by Macdonald), can often provide more information.

In order to see and assess Big Books before purchasing, telephone the publishers and ask for their representatives to put on a display of samples for your school. Publishers who publish Big Books include: Belitha Books, Collins Educational, Evans Brothers Ltd, Kingscourt Publications, Longman, Macdonald Children's Books, Newbridge Science, Oxford University Press, Random House, Rigby Heinemann, Scholastic Children's Books and Walker Books. Most LEA teachers' centres and children's libraries will have Big Book collections that you can look at and take out on loan. Specialist children's bookshops, educational suppliers and large stores belonging to major chains such as Ottakars also stock them. Heath Educational Books will supply an extensive list of titles and has a Teachers' Showroom in Surrey for groups or individual teachers to visit.

USING BIG BOOKS

It is now well-recognized that teaching literacy from a book large enough for a whole class to see not only imitates the closeness of a one-to-one relationship between

adult and child, but also has the additional benefit of giving everyone a chance to discuss the text in a wider group and tap into the ideas and perceptions of others.

Discussion about Big Book fiction can focus on features such as conventions of print, structure, settings, style, character, plot and author. Very young children can be made aware of devices used to build atmosphere and tension when they share *A Dark, Dark Tale* by Ruth Brown (published by Andersen Press). They can even appreciate dramatic irony and begin to think about things from different points of view when they consider the progress of a pig unwittingly being pursued by a wolf across the pages of *Suddenly!* by Colin McNaughton (Collins).

Poetry Big Books can be used to develop an awareness of rhythm and rhyme, and an appreciation of descriptive language. With non-fiction texts, children can be shown how the information is organized and taught how to access it. At sentence level, work on Big Books provides a way for the teacher to draw attention to features such as punctuation and sentence construction, and to encourage appropriate expression and intonation in reading aloud. At word level, the teaching opportunities for building up children's alphabetical knowledge and phonological awareness, pointing out common spelling patterns, and extending sight vocabulary are almost endless.

STORAGE AND DISPLAY

To keep Big Books in good condition, it is worth buying specially designed racks and display stands. Desk-top easels are useful as well as those designed to stand on the

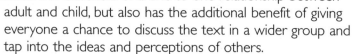

floor. Plastic hang-up bags can be obtained to protect books that are not in use. It is worth looking in library supplies catalogues such as LFC and Gresswells for these, or contact specialists such as Heron Educational or Teacher Boards.

THE ACTIVITY IDEAS

This book has been organized with the Literacy Hour in mind, and all the suggested activities have language teaching objectives. To fit in with schemes of work based on the Literacy Strategy, the activities have been grouped to deal separately with fiction, poetry and non-fiction texts.

A large number of activities could also be used in the teaching of other subjects, especially art and design. In these cases, the instructions include a sub-heading to this effect after the list of objectives.

Most of the activities in the non-fiction section also have cross-curricular links, but these have not been noted when they depend on the topic that the teacher chooses to focus on. The skills list provides a quick overview of the content of each activity.

Book-making suggestions have been included with the activities where appropriate. Teachers who wish to develop the paper engineering and design side of these may find inspiration in the workshops run by Paul Johnson, who has also written some very imaginative and helpful books on the subject, for example *Making Books* (published by A&C Black).

It has been taken for granted that teachers will already be well practised in the most important activity of all: that of reading books with the children again and again for sheer pleasure.

Based on the study of a variety of Big Book fiction texts, the activities in this section aim to develop children's understanding of:
■ plot structure and the sequence of events in different stories
■ character and role-play
■ how to identify and punctuate sentences
■ story settings and positional language
■ how to use a known story as a model for writing
■ how to reflect on and review their reading.

UNDERSTANDING COVER INFORMATION

OBJECTIVES

To enable children to:
■ understand information provided on the book cover
■ learn or revise the vocabulary 'title', 'author' and 'illustrator'
■ make predictions based on information given on the book cover.

RESOURCES AND CLASSROOM ORGANIZATION

You will need: a Big Book with a lively and interesting cover illustration. The author and illustrator should be named on the cover in large, clear print. For the whole-class teaching have a board or flip chart ready and three strips of paper or card labelled

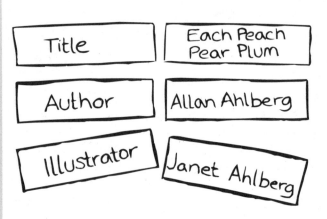

with the words 'title', 'author' and 'illustrator', and three strips with the actual title and author's and illustrator's names from the Big Book. You will also need some Blu-Tack to attach the strips to the board. Each child will need a copy of photocopiable page 22 and a pencil.

Children work as a class and then complete photocopiable page 22 individually or in pairs.

WHAT TO DO

Introduce the Big Book by discussing the picture on the cover. Ask the class what they notice. Extend positional vocabulary (above, below, beside, left, right) by asking the children to describe where objects are in the picture. Write some of their responses on the board to be used later as a wordbank for the writing task.

Point to and read the title of the book and ask the children to repeat it. Explain what the word 'title' means, and ask for other examples of book titles. Then explain the words 'author' and 'illustrator', and read out these names from the Big Book. Show the class the three prepared cards with the words 'title', 'author' and 'illustrator' on them. Ask three children to read out these words as you hold up the cards. Choose three more children to come out, in turn, for the three name cards and match each name with its partner from the first set. Read out each pair of words with the class. Attach the cards to the board for the children to refer to later.

6

Ready to go! IDEAS FOR USING BIG BOOKS

Finally, ask the children what they think is going to happen in the story and why. Are their predictions logical? How effectively are they able to use the information that they have? Refer them back to any hints provided by the cover illustration and title.

Read out the blurb on the back cover if there is one. Discuss the language of the blurb. Does it make them want to look inside or read the book? Ask the children whether looking at the covers of books helps them to choose books that they will like? Do book covers always give the right ideas about what is inside?

NOW OR LATER
■ Children could complete photocopiable page 22, either on their own or in mixed-ability pairs. Those who are unable to write without support could draw a picture in answer to the cover and prediction questions.
■ This activity can be repeated with other books in the classroom during guided or group reading sessions or by children individually.
■ Children could design their own covers and blurbs for home-made books.

WHAT COMES NEXT?

OBJECTIVES
To enable children to:
■ predict outcomes based on what has gone before
■ imitate the language and style of a particular book.

CROSS-CURRICULAR LINKS
DESIGN AND TECHNOLOGY
Plan the layout of an illustrated page.

ART
Make illustrations that complement the text and match the style of the pictures in the book.

RESOURCES AND CLASSROOM ORGANIZATION
You will need: a suitable Big Book as a stimulus, and a board or flip chart for modelling writing in front of the whole class. Each child will need paper and pencils for writing, and coloured crayons or paints for making illustrations.

Children work as a class, then in pairs of mixed ability or individually according to age.

WHAT TO DO
Choose a story with a clear repeating pattern. Traditional tales such as 'The Fisherman and his Wife', 'The Gingerbread Man' or 'The Little Red Hen' would be ideal. Read enough of the story for the children to recognize that there is a pattern in the way that the plot develops as well as in the language that is used. Stop reading before the end of the story. Ask the children what they have noticed about the things that keep recurring in the story so far. What actions are repeated? What words do the characters keep saying? Read the story extract again, and ask individual children to point out and say aloud the words and phrases that make up the pattern of the narrative.

For reinforcement with younger children, these words and phrases could be written out on cards to be held up and matched like snap cards as they recognize them in the story. The cards could also be used as a wordbank later when the children write their own version of the next page.

When it is clear that the children understand and recognize the repeating patterns in the story, ask them to give their own suggestions for words that might be written on the next page of the book. Write some suggestions on the board or flip chart. Ask one child to re-read the last page that you read. Which of the children's ideas sound best when you put them after what is actually written in the book? Discuss with the class why this is the case. For example, they may have used some of the same words as the original text, recognized and copied the pattern of the story, used the same characters, kept to the same tense, the same narrative voice and so on.

Ask the children how they would illustrate their text to make their own pictures like those in the book. Establish what they would they need to make the characters and background look the same as those in the story. What would they include? What colours would they use? What materials? Where on the page would they place their drawings?

NOW OR LATER

■ Working in pairs of mixed ability, children could discuss and draft the text that they think might be on the next page of the book, and then sketch their ideas for the layout and illustrations.

■ Alternatively, you could give the children a fresh start by reading the next page, comparing the actual events of the story with their predictions, and then asking them to imagine what might be written on the page after that.

■ Very young children could simply make drawings to show what they think might happen on the next page.

OBSERVING BASIC PUNCTUATION

OBJECTIVES

To enable children to:
■ note the use of punctuation marks in the text
■ understand how punctuation marks help with reading
■ distinguish between statements, questions and exclamations (older children)
■ begin to use punctuation marks in their own writing.

RESOURCES AND CLASSROOM ORGANIZATION

You will need: a Big Book with longish chunks of text containing plenty of examples of the punctuation that you wish to teach. With younger children, this could be very simple text that does not go beyond capital letters and full stops; for older children it could also include exclamation marks, question marks, commas and speech marks.

Use off-cuts from Post-it notes and cover up all the full stops in the text on a double-page spread. Have three A4 cards ready marked with a full stop, an exclamation mark and a question mark for the children to use in the extension activity. Use

photocopiable page 23 for individual children or pairs to consolidate the work on the three sentence types.

Children work as a class and then individually or in pairs.

WHAT TO DO

Read the story to the class up to the double-page spread where you have covered up the full stops. Now ask the children to spot the difference as you then read the marked extract in a suitably expressionless voice, without any pauses. Why did the extract sound boring and hard to understand? Can they tell you what has been covered over? Uncover each full stop, one at a time, demonstrating how different the text now sounds as the punctuation is put back into it.

Explain that punctuation helps people to make sense of what they read, and also makes the story sound more interesting. Turn over and repeat the process with a different extract, this time hiding the full stops with the help of individual children. Demonstrate again how difficult it is to read, and talk about the part that each full stop plays in dividing up the text and showing how it should be read.

SUGGESTIONS FOR SUPPORT AND EXTENSION

Children who need further practice in identifying full stops could listen again as you re-read the story, carefully following the words as you do so, and clapping once each time they recognize a full stop. Point out how each sentence begins with a capital letter. Repeat the activity as you read successive pages.

Older or more able children could go on to focus on the different effects of full stops, question marks and exclamation marks on meaning and intonation. Draw attention to examples of these in a Big Book and discuss with the children how they affect the reading of the story. Show how both the question mark and the exclamation mark contain, and have the strength of, a full stop.

Introduce (or revise) the concept that some sentences take the form of statements, while others are questions or exclamations. Each type of sentence has a matching mark at the end of it. Explain to the children that if they listen carefully, they will hear the differences between the way that the three types of sentences sound. Use Post-It notes to cover up examples of each of the three types of punctuation marks in the Big Book, and have the three A4 cards with the punctuation marks on them to hand. As you read aloud to the class, ask individual children to guess which punctuation mark goes where. Give them the appropriate card to hold up, and test whether they are right by re-reading the sentence as if it ended with the mark that is on the card.

This activity could also be applied to the identification of commas and speech marks in other Big Book texts.

NOW OR LATER

■ Children could work individually or in pairs to complete photocopiable page 23, sharing their own ideas for questions with the rest of the class when they have finished.

■ As an additional activity, children could proof-read a story extract which has the basic punctuation marks omitted from the narrative.

WORKING WITH SENTENCES

RESOURCES AND CLASSROOM ORGANIZATION

You will need: a Big Book text that is written in straightforward sentences. Avoid stories that include quotation marks or speech bubbles, as these could confuse the children at first. Many information books, as well as fiction texts, would be suitable for the sentence-spotting activity.

Prepare nine A4 size cards or sheets of paper marked out as shown below, and have some Blu-Tack so that you can put up the cards where they can be seen later. Each child will need pencils and a copy of photocopiable page 24.

OBJECTIVES

To enable children to:
■ identify sentences within a text
■ understand that a sentence should make sense
■ construct and punctuate sentences.

Children work as a class for the initial discussion about sentences and then complete the photocopiable sheet working individually or in pairs.

WHAT TO DO

Begin by asking the children if they know what a sentence is. Revise or explain that it is a group of words that starts with a capital letter and ends with a full stop. Make sure that the children understand the difference between capital and lower-case letters by referring to the Big Book or to signs and notices in the classroom. Show them the A4 card with the full stop on it to remind them what a full stop looks like. Explain that the words in a sentence ought to make sense. Tell the children that they are going to try to build up a sentence with the cards that you have made.

Ask individual children to come out, one after the other, and hold up each card in turn in front of the class. Every time a card is added to the word chain, ask whether the words now make sense and form a sentence. Rearrange the children so that the sentence makes sense. When the sentence is complete, ask a volunteer to come out and finish it off with the full stop.

Show the class the Big Book that you have chosen. Read a short extract and then ask the children to re-read it and point out the sentences. If possible, assign individual children a sentence each to read aloud to the class, reinforcing the idea of capital letters and full stops as 'start' and 'finish' signals.

Explain to the children that they are now going to write some sentences of their own on photocopiable page 24. They have been given the first few words to start them off but they have to think of some words of their own to complete each sentence. When they have finished, they should look for some sentences in the Big Book and copy them out carefully.

SUGGESTIONS FOR SUPPORT AND EXTENSION

Less able pupils could be given word cards with which to form short, simple sentences and then copy them out. More able children could go on to compose their own sentences on a set topic without further support.

NOW OR LATER

■ This work could be linked with 'Observing basic punctuation' on page 8, in which the focus is on observation of punctuation in general.

SEQUENCING EVENTS

OBJECTIVES

To enable children to:
■ observe the order of events in a story
■ put events in chronological order
■ use a simple number sequence.

CROSS-CURRICULAR LINKS

MATHS

Sequencing numbers and understanding chronological order.

RESOURCES AND CLASSROOM ORGANIZATION

Choose a Big Book story with a clear sequential pattern. Cumulative tales such as 'The Gingerbread Man' or traditional stories based on the 'rule of three' pattern such as 'The Three Billy Goats Gruff' or 'Goldilocks and the Three Bears' would be ideal.

Prepare a summary of the story in a sequence of simple sentences and/or pictures. These should be photocopied onto A4 paper or card and then cut apart for the children to use. Photocopiable page 25 (which accompanies the activity 'Finding the plot', page 11) could be used if you decide to draw a sequence of pictures. If possible, make an A3 size enlargement of both the sentence sheet and the picture sheet to show to the class. Have writing materials available.

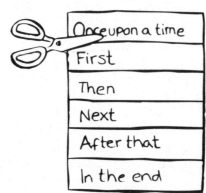
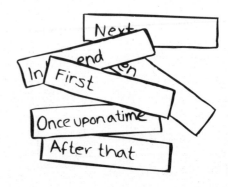

Children work as a class for the story reading and subsequent discussion about the activity. They then work in pairs or small groups to arrange and number the text or picture cards in the correct sequence.

WHAT TO DO

Tell the children that you are going to read them a new story, then 'play dumb' by opening the Big Book somewhere in the middle and starting to read. When the children protest, reinforce the idea that a story makes complete sense only if it is read from the beginning. Start the story again and read it through from the beginning to the end. Now show the children the enlarged versions of the jumbled sentence, or picture cards, that you have prepared. Tell them that you are going to use these to retell the story. Ask them to identify which card should go at the beginning and which at the end. Write a 1 on the first card and number the final card appropriately. Talk about the sequence of numbers that the children will need to put in for themselves between the first and last cards. Link the vocabulary of number and order: 'We need to put a 1 first, then a 2 second. What will come third?' and so on.

Give each pair or group of children a set of cards and ask them to lay them out in the correct sequence and then label them in numerical order. When all the children have finished sorting their cards, ask them to check the correct sequence of events by referring back to the Big Book.

SUGGESTIONS FOR SUPPORT AND EXTENSION

Younger and less able children could be given pictures to sequence instead of sentences. They could peg the pictures in order across a 'washing line' or stick numbers on to them to show the order of events.

More able children could work independently and write sentences describing the beginning, middle and ending of other stories.

NOW OR LATER

This activity provides useful preparation for further exploration of story structure, and could be used as an introduction to work on making storyboards ('Finding the plot', see below) and story maps ('Setting the scene', page 17).

FINDING THE PLOT

RESOURCES AND CLASSROOM ORGANIZATION

You will need: a Big Book with a very simple story plot for sequencing and storyboarding activities. Many traditional tales are far more complicated than you might think – imagine all the frames you would need to make a storyboard of the key events in a story such as 'Cinderella' or 'Puss-in-Boots'! A clearly structured sequential story such as *The Very Hungry Caterpillar* by Eric Carle (published by Longman) or simple versions of tales with repeating story patterns such as 'The Three Little Pigs' or 'The Fisherman and his Wife' work best to begin with. Fables such as 'The Boy Who Cried Wolf' would also be suitable.

Have some examples of comic strips to show to the children, and a board or flip chart ready marked into nine sections in the same way as photocopiable page 25. The photocopiable sheet itself should be used by children for the storyboard activity. They will need pencils and crayons. Provide sketchbooks if they are used to drafting ideas for pictures in these.

OBJECTIVES

To enable the children to:
■ begin to understand how stories are structured
■ sequence events in chronological order
■ plot key events on storyboards.

CROSS-CURRICULAR LINKS

MATHS

Sequence numbers and events across lines and grids.

ART

Illustrate characters and events.

| Once upon a time there were three little pigs. | The first pig built a house of straw. | The second pig built a house of twigs. | The third pig built a house of bricks. |

Children work as a class for the story reading and subsequent discussion, and then work individually to complete the photocopiable sheet.

WHAT TO DO

Read the whole story to the class until they are familiar with the plot. Discuss how the story begins and ends, and what happens in the middle. Refer back to the Big Book to help the children to recall the sequence of events. As you go back over the story, introduce a variety of 'time' vocabulary into the discussion (first, in the beginning, at the start, next, later on, after this, then, when, at last, finally, in the end). Explain that the children are going to retell the story in the form of a cartoon or comic strip. They will only have nine spaces for their pictures, so they will have to decide very carefully what they think are the most important parts of the story. Discuss what they might draw in the first frame, and what they think the last picture should be. What captions might they write under their pictures? Model some of their suggestions for drawings and captions on the prepared board or flip chart.

The children should now work individually to make their own storyboards on photocopiable page 25, trying out their ideas in sketchbooks first if appropriate.

SUGGESTIONS FOR SUPPORT AND EXTENSION

Less able children could write one-word captions for their drawings, while the more able could write sentences. You could draw and write in the first box on the photocopiable sheet to give the children a start.

NOW OR LATER

■ If the children enjoyed this activity, ask them to retell other stories in comic-strip format.
■ Try using a different number of frames and/or larger paper. Vary the layout by, for example, using a horizontal strip or a zigzag book in place of a grid.
■ Suggest that they include speech bubbles with the characters in their pictures.

| The wolf blew down the house of straw. | Then he blew down the house of twigs. |

WHO'S WHO?

RESOURCES AND CLASSROOM ORGANIZATION

You will need: a Big Book with clearly defined good and bad characters. Many traditional tales will be appropriate. For example, 'Cinderella', 'Hansel and Gretel', 'Little Red Riding Hood'. You will also need a board or flip chart for note taking during the question and answer session. Each child will need a pencil, crayons and a copy of photocopiable page 26 for the follow-up work.

Children work initially as a class and then in groups or individually.

WHAT TO DO

After reading the story with the children several times so that they know it well, ask them who it is about, writing a list on the board or flip chart. Explain that the people (or animals) in a story are called characters. Discuss how characters are imaginary and therefore different from real people or animals. Then ask the class about the characters that you have listed. Can they describe the appearance of each character: how would they recognize them if they were to meet them? Ask the children to refer back to the book for details about how each character looks and dresses. Write down their descriptions so the children can refer to them later.

Now discuss how the different characters in your list behave and write down suggestions for suitable adjectives to describe their personalities (*kind, helpful, clever, strong, brave, hardworking, mean, selfish, cruel, greedy, cunning, silly*). For each suggestion, prompt the children to go back to the story by asking questions: *How do we know that? What did he or she do or say to make you think that?* Find the relevant passages and point out the evidence to the whole class ('Cinderella is hardworking' – we know that she works hard because we can see her on this page sweeping the floor). Discuss which characteristics that the children have identified are good and which are bad.

Tell the children that they are going to play a game called 'Guess Who?'. The idea is to think of a character from the Big Book story and describe his or her behaviour and appearance without saying who the character is. The children then have to guess who it is. Start the game yourself and then involve the children as they become confident with the idea. Once the game is in progress, whoever is the first to guess correctly can present the next description.

Follow up this activity by asking the children to complete photocopiable page 26. This could be done in groups or individually according to ability.

He wears a gold crown.
He likes dancing.
He wants to marry a girl with glass slippers.

NOW OR LATER

■ Completed photocopiable sheets could be mounted to form a wall display, or slipped back-to-back into an A4 display folder to make a class book for the children to share.
■ Repeat the 'Guess Who?' game with other Big Books and stories.
■ Children could draw a particular character and then label him or her using adjectives from a wordbank. See the illustration at the top of page 14.

See the illustration at the top of page 14.

OBJECTIVES
To enable children to:
■ understand the word 'character'
■ list the characters from a simple story
■ describe the appearance and behaviour of the characters with reference to the text.

Puss-in-boots

brave

cunning

loyal

smart

a liar

clever

kind

helpful

WHO SAYS WHAT?

OBJECTIVES

To enable children to:
■ role-play different characters
■ develop clarity, fluency and expression in reading
■ use art and drama to envisage characters and settings.

CROSS-CURRICULAR LINKS

DESIGN AND TECHNOLOGY

Plan and make a miniature scene inside a shoebox; design and make puppets and/or masks.

ART

Draw, colour and cut out scenery and characters.

RESOURCES AND CLASSROOM ORGANIZATION

You will need: a Big Book written in a play format. Some good examples are published by Heinemann in their *Magic Bean* series. Alternatively, choose a conventional story which contains substantial sections of dialogue. Begin by exploring the story with the whole class. Have some simple percussion instruments available to add sound effects to the reading.

Children work initially as a class and then individually or in small groups for the reading activity. The art and design activities which follow would probably be best done individually or in small groups. Each child will need empty shoeboxes (or similar), paper, card, string for masks, sticks for puppets, pencils, paints or crayons, scissors, glue, adhesive tape and a variety of craft materials such as scraps of cloth, wool, ribbon and foil.

WHAT TO DO

Read the story or extract to the children, pointing out when different characters are speaking. Ask the children which characters have spoken. How can they tell who said what? Make sure that they understand the conventions of layout used for writing dialogue. Divide the class so that individual children read out the different parts. You could involve shy or less able children by asking them to read out their parts in groups.

Work on developing appropriate expression. As the children become confident in speaking the dialogue, encourage them to add movements and sound effects to the 'performance'. Hot-seat individual children to explore the motives and feelings of different characters. Ask them questions: *Why did you do that? How did you feel when…?* Arrange the children into groups and ask each group to arrange itself into a 'freeze-frame', or still 'photograph', to illustrate a key scene. For example, Cinderella trying on the glass slipper at home the day after the ball.

14

NOW OR LATER

■ Groups of children could act out different scenes from the play, or story, and then give performances to the rest of the class. Before they begin, sort out who will say what. Children who lack the confidence to speak could mime to a narrator or provide sound effects. Groups could be guided by classroom assistants or parent helpers if these are available.

■ Transform the dialogue into a puppet play. Children could draw their characters on to card, then cut them out and use colour and collage (wool for hair, paper or cloth for clothes) to enliven their appearance. Finish by taping the characters to sticks (short canes designed to support pot plants are ideal). A table top or large box-frame could be used for staging.

■ Show children how to design and make simple masks to wear during their performance. Use photocopiable page 27 as a basic template, referring to the Big Book to add ears, hair or a crown as appropriate. Help the children to mark the positions of their eyes and mouths

Make a hole in the centre.

Cut outwards from the hole.

Cut around inner edges of outline.

(they should press on to the outside of the mask to indicate these), and demonstrate how to make 'star' cuts to cut out shapes for eyes and mouth.

■ Children could try to envisage a particular scene from the play in three-dimensional detail. They could work in pairs to create a mini-stage set inside a shoebox, using paper, card, Plasticine and scrap materials to make scenery, props and characters. Alternatively, the scene could be created with the help of doll's house furnishings, toys or LEGO.

15

Ready to go! IDEAS FOR USING BIG BOOKS

READING THE PICTURES

OBJECTIVES
To enable children to:
■ develop positional language
■ ask and answer relevant questions
■ enhance awareness of initial letter sounds
■ understand some of the ways in which pictures can enrich a text.

CROSS-CURRICULAR LINKS
ART
Appreciation of book design and illustration.

RESOURCES AND CLASSROOM ORGANIZATION

You will need: a Big Book with highly detailed illustrations, such as *A Country Far Away* by Philippe Dupasquier and Nigel Gray (a wonderful picture book contrasting the lifestyle of a boy growing up in a Sudanese village with that of a child in suburban Britain, published by Andersen Press), or *Each Peach, Pear, Plum* by Janet and Allan Ahlberg (published by Viking).

Have a wordbank of positional vocabulary prepared on a board or flip chart for the children to refer to. This should contain words such as: *in, on, over, under, above, below, beside, next to, among, left, right, behind, in front of, at the back of, middle, corner, edge, centre, bottom, top*. To support the less able children prepare some simple sentences with the positional words missing and write the missing words on cards.

Children work initially as a class, and then in pairs or small groups to complete the activity.

WHAT TO DO

Read the text to the class, and then ask them to look very carefully at the pictures in the Big Book. What do they notice? Use each response to develop positional language by asking the child to describe the exact place of the object on the page. For example, not simply 'I can see a boy waving goodbye', but 'I can see a boy waving goodbye. He is standing in the bottom right-hand corner of the picture, facing the bus.' Use the wordbank that you have prepared to help the children find the words that they need. When most of the children appear to have understood this idea, confident writers could go on to write sentences about 'A Handful of Objects', noting the position of five things that they can see in the picture.

SUGGESTIONS FOR SUPPORT AND EXTENSION

Less able writers could be given simple sentences with gaps in which to place positional words. Write down the words that they will need on cards. Alternatively, they could draw simple pictures to show their understanding of positional words. For example, 'The cat is under the table'.

More able pupils could extend their sentences by adding further descriptive detail: 'I can see a boy waving goodbye. He is standing in the bottom right-hand corner of the picture, facing the bus. He has a school bag under one arm and he is wearing a green jumper.'

NOW OR LATER

■ Reinforce the children's concepts of initial sounds by playing games of 'I-Spy' with the pictures in Big Books.
■ Change the 'Handful of Objects' idea to a 'Handful of Questions' that the children have to make up about the things that they notice in the picture. Provide a framework for this activity by giving the children a different word with which to start each question. Their questions could be recorded on paper or shared orally with the rest of the class.

SETTING THE SCENE

RESOURCES AND CLASSROOM ORGANIZATION

You will need: a Big Book in which the narrative moves to a variety of locations to help the children understand where different places are in the story. They should have some idea of what a map looks like already: non-fiction Big Books (Heinemann and Wayland both publish books about maps for KS1) could be used to develop this, as well as Big Book versions of stories such as *Rosie's Walk* by Pat Hutchins (published by Puffin) or *Katie Morag and the Two Grandmothers* by Mairi Hedderwick (published by Red Fox). Both these titles show a picture map of the story setting before the narrative begins.

To help the children to make their own maps you will need a Big Book such as *We're Going on a Bear Hunt* by Michael Rosen and Helen Oxenbury or *Handa's Surprise* by Eileen Browne (both published by Walker Books) in which the children can visualize for themselves the character's journey from place to place.

Have large sheets of paper available, together with pencils and paints or crayons. Use a board or flip chart to sketch out ideas in front of the class. Prepare cards for less able pupils naming and/or sketching each location that occurs in the story.

Children work initially as a class with the Big Book and for the subsequent discussion about maps. They then work individually or in pairs to draw their own maps.

WHAT TO DO

Show the children a variety of simple maps and discuss with them how maps show the location of different places. Have the children seen or used maps outside school? Discuss the examples that they suggest, and how they are used. Talk about the ways in which maps can help people to find their way if they are going on a journey.

Read the story with the class until they know it well. Explain that you want the children to make their own maps of the journey that takes place in the story. Go back to the beginning and ask the

OBJECTIVES
To enable children to:
■ visualize the places in a story
■ follow the movement of a character from one place to another
■ make a simple map.

CROSS-CURRICULAR LINKS
ART
Draw a sketch map; make a three-dimensional model.

GEOGRAPHY
Develop concepts of location and direction.

17

children to name the place where the story begins. Write the location on the board or flip chart. Referring to the book each time, ask the children to list, one after the other, the different locations as they occur in the story. Write these down on the board to be used as an aide-memoire: the children will need to remember to include all the locations in their maps, and also put them in the right order.

Model the drawing of a sketch map by asking individual children to come out and make quick sketches of the various places on your list. Ask other children to label each place. When most children seem confident with the idea, set them to sketch their own maps of the story working either individually or in pairs.

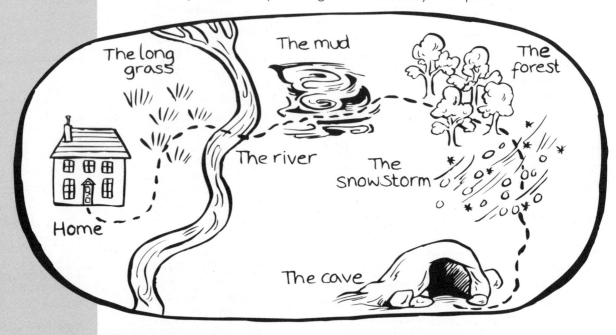

SUGGESTIONS FOR SUPPORT AND EXTENSION

Less able children could be supported by being given ready-made cards with the names and/or sketches of all the places in the story. These could be sorted and then sequenced across the drawing paper from left to right. More able children could add a key to their maps.

NOW OR LATER

■ Finished maps could be used as the basis of three-dimensional models. These could be made out of various combinations of card, twigs, junk materials, modelling materials such as Plasticine or clay, construction kits such as LEGO, and toy animals, people and cars.

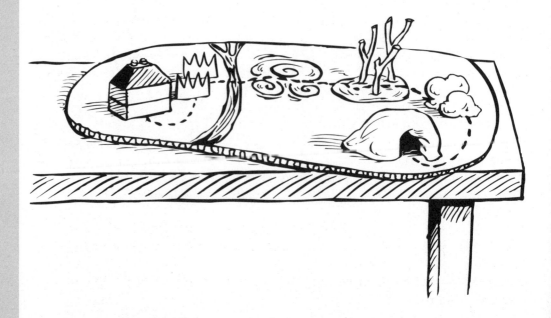

CHANGING THE STORY

OBJECTIVES
To enable children to:
■ develop vocabulary
■ understand story structure
■ use a known story as a model for creating a new version.

RESOURCES AND CLASSROOM ORGANIZATION

You will need: a Big Book with a simple, clearly patterned story structure. The examples that follow are based on *We're Going on a Bear Hunt* by Michael Rosen and Helen Oxenbury (published by Walker Books) and the traditional story of 'Goldilocks and the Three Bears'. Use cut-down Post-it notes to cover over all the words that refer to characters and settings. Have a board or flip chart ready on which to note down words that are suggested by the class during the discussion. Each child will need pencils and copies of photocopiable page 28.

Children work as a class for the Big Book story and subsequent discussion. When planning their own stories on the photocopiable sheet they should work in pairs of mixed ability.

This activity is best suited to older pupils in KS1.

WHAT TO DO

Read the story to the class several times until they have become familiar with all the details. Tell the children that you are now going to help them to write their own version of the story, in which the main ideas will stay the same, but some of the details will be different. Explain what a 'version' is by referring to examples such as Babette Cole's reworking of Cinderella in *Prince Cinders* (published by Puffin) or *The Three Little Wolves and the Big Bad Pig* by E. Trivizas (Mammoth Books).

Show the children the Big Book again, but this time with all the words that refer to characters and settings covered over. Begin with the characters. Ask for suggestions as to how these could be changed. For example, in 'Goldilocks and the Three Bears', the character of Goldilocks could be changed to a boy and the bears could become different animals. *What about a new version called 'Jonathan and the Three Gorillas'?* Now go on to change the settings. *Where could the gorillas live instead of a cottage? What might they sit on instead of chairs?* If you take the example of *We're Going on a Bear Hunt*, the title could be changed to *We're Going on a Lion Hunt* and the various places passed on the journey – long grass, river and mud – changed to different locations such as on an aeroplane, across a desert, under some palm trees and so on.

When you have thoroughly discussed ideas for alternative characters and settings with the children, they should then work together in pairs to make their own plans on photocopiable page 28.

> We could make Goldilocks into a boy!

> And the three bears could be gorillas.

SUGGESTIONS FOR SUPPORT

To give the children extra support with their planning, you could write in the details of the original story for them on the photocopiable sheet, so that all they need to do is note down their own ideas for changes.

NOW OR LATER

■ Pairs of children could read out their plans to the rest of the class.
■ They could go on to write their new versions of the story using their planning sheets.
■ Their stories could be compiled into a book and placed in the class library for everyone to share.

RETELLING ALOUD

OBJECTIVES

To enable children to:
■ recall events in sequence
■ develop confidence in speaking
■ show the actions suggested by stories.

RESOURCES AND CLASSROOM ORGANIZATION

You will need: a fiction Big Book with a clear, uncomplicated plot. For younger children a story with a repeating pattern would be best. You could also make up a 'story bag' of props for the children to use as prompts: dolls, toy animals and other small objects that occur in the story. For example, if you were to make up a 'story bag' for *Dogger* by Shirley Hughes (published by Red Fox, a well-known tale of a boy who loses his much loved toy dog in a moment of distraction), you could put in an old toy dog, a pull-along trolley, string, a small blanket, a cardboard ice-cream cone (the object that causes the distraction in the story) and so on.

There are ready-made toys available for purchase that accompany some Big Book stories, for example the *Elmer* stories by David McKee (published by Andersen Press) and *Stellaluna* by Janell Cannon (published by D. Bennett books). Alternatively, a set of simple picture prompts prepared in advance on large card would remind the children of the order of events.

This activity begins with the children working as a class with the Big Book in front of them. For the retelling activity they should sit in a circle, in smaller groups, so that the atmosphere is less intimidating and each child can have one of the props or pictures to handle. However, each group will still need your support or that of a parent or adult helper.

WHAT TO DO

Read and re-read the story to the children until they become familiar with all the details. Explain that they (or a group of them) are now going to move into a circle and take turns to tell the story to one another without the book. Start by asking an articulate child how the story begins. Help the children to continue telling the story around the circle by showing or handing them the props or picture prompts. Encourage them to add actions to the words if appropriate. For example, 'Dave pulled Dogger along on a lead made of string. When it was cold he wrapped him in a blanket.'

NOW OR LATER

■ Having retold the story in this way, groups of children could go on to prepare retellings of other Big Book stories to present to the rest of the class. With your help, they could look carefully through the books and choose simple props that they could make to put into their own 'story bags'.

■ Divide the class into groups to enact and retell different parts of a familiar Big Book story. For example, with *We're Going on a Bear Hunt* the children could be divided up so that a different group describes and acts out the encounter with each obstacle on the journey: the struggle through the long grass (*Swishy, swashy!*); the wading through the deep cold river (*Splash splosh!*) and so on. This type of dramatized retelling could be practised and then performed to other classes.

REVIEWING THE STORY

RESOURCES AND CLASSROOM ORGANIZATION

You will need: a Big Book that the children have enjoyed reading with you. There should be more than one character in the story. Have a flip chart or board ready to write on as you discuss the story with the children. For their work on photocopiable page 29, the Big Book should be nearby (or normal size copies if they are available) for the children to refer to as they draw and write. As it is intended that the photocopiable sheet should be folded down the centre to form the inside of a booklet, you may prefer to copy it onto card rather than paper.

Children work initially as a class and then individiually to complete the photocopiable sheet.

WHAT TO DO

With the Big Book nearby for reference, discuss with the children what they thought of the story. Did things turn out in the way that they expected? If not, what happened that surprised them? Which part of the story did they like best? Can they explain why? Ask them to recall and describe the different characters in the story (see 'Who's who?', page 13). Write the characters' names on the board or chart. Which character would they most like to meet in real life? Again, encourage them to give reasons for their choices. Talk about the illustrations in the book. If they could have a copy of any one picture to take home and put on their wall, which one would it be? What do they like about the particular illustrations that they have chosen?

Finally, discuss the vocabulary used in the story. Have they learned any new words through reading the book? Which words can they still hear in their heads? Find some of the words that they suggest in the book. Copy them out and read them aloud with the class joining in.

Now give each child photocopiable page 29 to complete. Tell them that they are each going to write and draw their own review of the book in a little booklet for the whole class to read. Make sure that everyone understands that this means looking back through the story and giving their opinions about it. When they have completed the inside section of the booklet, the children can illustrate and label the cover:

My review of…
by…

NOW OR LATER

■ Children can read out their reviews and show their booklets to one another.
■ Using or adapting this format, children could make reviews of other books that they have enjoyed reading. Their finished booklets could be displayed in covered shoeboxes or empty plastic ice-cream boxes for the class to read.

OBJECTIVES

To enable children to:
■ think about the contents of the book
■ express opinions
■ give reasons for their opinions.

Photocopiables

Looking at a book cover

The title of the book is

_____

The author is

_____

The illustrator is

_____

In the cover picture I can see

What I think will happen in the story is

Photocopiables

What goes where?

| This is a full stop. | This is a question mark. | This is an exclamation mark. |

■ Choose which one to put at the end of these sentences:

1. What day is it today

2. I am going to play with my friend after school

3. Come here at once

4. How old are you

5. What would you like to eat

6. When are we going home

7. Don't run across the road

8. Once upon a time there were three little pigs

■ Now think of some questions of your own. They have been started for you.

What _____?

How _____?

When _____?

Photocopiables

Writing sentences

■ Write your own ending for each of these sentences:

1. Once upon a time _____

_____

2. I like _____

_____

3. I don't like_____

_____

4. This morning, I_____

_____

5. We went to_____

_____

6. When I get home, I_____

_____

■ Now find some sentences in the book and write them in this space:

Photocopiables

My storyboard of _____

The Photocopiables

Describing a character

Name_____

Age_____

Sex_____

■ Draw a picture of your character in the box:

How they look _____

_____

_____

_____

Things they do_____

_____

_____

_____

Things they say_____

_____

_____

Photocopiables

Shape for a mask

1. Cut out basic oval shape from card.

2. Check positions of child's eyes and mouth. Redraw on reverse of card if necessary.

5. Add nose, hair and ears.

4. Cut along dotted lines at temple and chin. Fold sides over one another and staple together for 3-D effect.

3. Cut out eyes and mouth starting from centre dots.

Ready to go! IDEAS FOR USING BIG BOOKS

Photocopiables

My plan for changing the story

Name of story_____

_____

New name of story_____

_____

Characters in the story　　　　　　　New characters

Places in the story　　　　　　　　　New places

Photocopiables

The words that I like the sound of are

My favourite picture is

Reviewing the story

The character that I would most like to meet is

because

The part of the story that I like best is

Using Big Book poetry books, nursery rhymes and stories with strong elements of rhythm and rhyme, the following activities are designed to help children to:
■ develop a sense of poetic language through the use of similes
■ identify patterns of rhythm and rhyme
■ compose their own rhymes and rhythmic sound patterns
■ become familiar with popular nursery rhymes
■ enjoy memorizing, reciting and acting out poems and rhymes.

A BOOK OF SIMILES

OBJECTIVES

To enable children to:
■ develop visual imagination
■ make and use similes
■ use poetic language.

CROSS-CURRICULAR LINKS

ART AND DESIGN
Design and colour illustrations.

RESOURCES AND CLASSROOM ORGANIZATION

You will need a Big Book which features simple and effective similes. This activity is based on the Big Book *Deep in a Rainforest* by Gwen Pascoe, (in the *Magic Beans* series published by Heinemann). It is not actually a poetry book, but more of an exploration of the colours and wildlife to be seen in a rainforest. If this book is not available, use another that features effective similes and adapt the brainstorming session and follow-up writing accordingly. Have a board or flip chart ready to write down suggestions during the brainstorming session that follows the shared reading. Before the lesson, write the heading: 'On a busy city street the world can be…' Also have available some pictures and information books about the 'world' that the children are going to write about.

The activity begins with whole-class shared reading, after which the children should work in pairs to produce their own simile on a page for a class book. The children will need pencils and coloured crayons, rough paper for drafting, and a large piece of thick paper or card between two for making their 'book' pages.

WHAT TO DO

Read the book with the children, pointing out the colours and similes as you do so.

Deep in a rainforest the world can be…
> *as red as a parrot*
> *as orange as a fungus*
> *as yellow as a flower.*

Make sure that the children understand what a simile is. If they are not familiar with the term, explain it and give some more examples. Then talk about a different 'world' such as a city, a desert or under an ocean. Ask the class how this place could be described in a similar way. Show the children pictures of the place that you have in mind and ask them about the colours that they can see. For example: *Can anyone suggest what red objects might be seen on a city street? What about a fire engine? As red as a fire engine?* Write suitable ideas on the board or flip chart. Continue the brainstorming by asking for suggestions of more colours, or introduce different adjectives, for example 'as shiny as a shop window', 'as loud as a lorry going past'.

Now ask each pair of children to write down and illustrate a simile about an object found in your chosen setting.

SUGGESTIONS FOR SUPPORT AND EXTENSION

Less able pupils could use the ideas already generated in the brainstorm. The rest of the class should work out their own ideas in rough first, and discuss them with you before writing them out and illustrating them ready to be put in a class book of similes. Quick finishers could design a cover for the book or produce more pages.

NOW OR LATER

Join the finished pages together by using a spiral binder, or by punching holes and making string hinges. Alternatively, use a ready-made clearview display folder and insert sheets of A4

paper or card into the plastic pockets back to back. Although this is a fairly expensive way of making a class book, the pages can easily be removed for the children to take home and the folder can be used repeatedly.

ORCHESTRATING RHYTHM

RESOURCES AND CLASSROOM ORGANIZATION

You will need: Big Books with a clear, repetitive sound pattern to the narrative. The activities that follow are based on *The Farm Concert* and *Sing a Song* both by Joy Cowley (in the *Story Chest* series published by Nelson) and *The Train Ride* by June Crebbin (Walker Books). Have a selection of simple percussion instruments available.

Initially the children work as a class and then in groups with the instruments. Finally, they will need pencils and copies of photocopiable page 40 to complete individually.

OBJECTIVES

To enable children to:
- observe syllables in words
- identify patterns of rhythm in poems
- repeat rhythmic sounds
- add music to rhythm.

CROSS-CURRICULAR LINKS

MUSIC
Use instruments to create rhythmic sound patterns.

WHAT TO DO

Introduce the activity by asking the children to clap out the syllables or beats that they can hear in words and sentences as you read them out. *Sing a Song* is an ideal book to use for this. It begins:

Sing, sing, sing a song,
Sing a song together.

This rythmic pattern is repeated to describe each subsequent activity of the tiger family in the evening routine that follows: *Come, come, come to tea. In, in, in the bath*, and so on.

When the children have understood the idea of clapping once for each syllable, try tapping, finger-snapping and vocal sounds, and then striking the percussion

instruments instead of clapping. Divide the class into groups to vary the accompanying sound effects according to different sections of the story. For example, one group could sing *La, la, la* instead of *Sing a song*; another group could strike a gong or chime-bars for *Come to tea*. The rest of the class could read the words from the Big Book with you as each group has its turn at supplying the sounds.

In *The Farm Concert*, a sequential story in which the animals' noises stop the farmer from sleeping until they lower their 'voices' to a whisper, the sound effects are already supplied in the text: *Moo-moo went the cow*; *Woof-woof went the dog*, and so on.

The six different animal sounds in this book could be allocated to six different groups of children, with an individual child reading the words of the farmer. If the children manage this easily, you could go on to do it as a round, starting with everyone making their group sounds all at once (very noisy), and ending with all whispering very softly.

Tell the children that they are now going to sort out some animal sounds for themselves and make a poem about a zoo. Give each child a copy of photocopiable page 40 to complete.

SUGGESTIONS FOR SUPPORT AND EXTENSION

The children could copy the appropriate sounds from the wordbank on the photocopiable sheet or cut them out and stick them where they fit. More able children could be given the sheet without reference to the wordbank and asked to think of suitable animal sounds by themselves.

NOW OR LATER

The Train Ride could be divided up in a similar way. Point out how the rhythm in this story sounds like the wheels of a train clanking along a railway track.

We're off on a journey
Out of the town –
What shall I see?
What shall I see?

Show the children how the page breaks in this story also indicate a difference in pace, with the basic rhythm pattern gradually building up as the train gathers speed.

If you use this book with children in Year 2, you could also read 'From a railway carriage' by Robert Louis Stevenson and see if they can hear the rhythm of the train in this poem as well.

RECOGNIZING RHYME

OBJECTIVES

To enable children to:
■ identify rhyming words
■ share their own ideas for rhymes
■ extend vocabulary
■ raise awareness of spelling
■ distinguish between different rhyming patterns.

RESOURCES AND CLASSROOM ORGANIZATION

You will need: a variety of Big Books of poetry. The range chosen should include poems with different rhyme schemes. The books specifically referred to in this activity are *Laughing Giraffes* (an anthology in the Literacy Links series published by Mimosa Publications) and *The Fish Who Could Wish* by John Bush, illustrated by Korky Paul (published by Oxford University Press). Have a board or flip chart available to write on during the brainstorming session. You will also need some Post-it notes to cover over both the rhyming words in the Big Book and for the guessing game.

Children work as a class initially and then individually to complete photocopiable page 41.

WHAT TO DO

Begin by reading a rhyming poem to the children and asking them to spot the words that rhyme. Write the rhyming pairs of words on the board or chart, leaving sufficient space to write under each pair. Now show the children the page or pages of the Big Book in which you have covered over some of the rhyming words. Discuss which words the children think would fit best in the spaces. Go on to brainstorm other words that rhyme with those that they have already identified, and list these in the appropriate columns. Ask the class to look at the spelling of the words in each list. *Do all the rhyming sounds have the same spelling? What different spellings are there for the same sounds? Which spellings are the most common?*

Next, play 'Guess the rhyme'. Show the children another rhyming poem in which you have blanked out some of the rhyming words, and ask them to guess what the missing words might be and how to spell them. Emphasize that their guesses will have to make sense as well as rhyme. Do not accept half-rhymes, as these will only confuse the object of the game.

Give out photocopiable page 41 and ask the children to guess the missing words and write them down. Explain that they should then try to make lists of other rhymes, as they have just done in the class. They can continue on the back of the sheet if they need more space.

NOW OR LATER

■ Ask the children to share their lists of rhymes with the rest of the class.
■ With pairs of children of similar ability, play the game of 'Word tennis' (a drama idea invented by Anna Scher). A pair of children stand up and take turns to call out different words with the same theme (in this instance, 'words that rhyme with…') until one of them runs out of ideas or repeats a word that has already been played.
■ Children could look at a selection of poems with different rhyme patterns and notice how their rhyme schemes work. For example, rhyming couplets in 'Ella McStumping', a poem by Michael Dugan (from *Laughing Giraffes*):

Ella McStumping
was fond of jumping.
From tables and chairs
Bookshelves and stairs.

■ Alternatively, find poems that rhyme at the end of alternate lines and occasionally within the same line, as in *The Fish Who Could Wish*:

In the deep blue sea
In the deep of the blue
Swam a fish who could wish
And each wish would come true.

WORKING WITH NURSERY RHYMES

OBJECTIVES

To enable children to:
■ identify nursery rhyme characters
■ explore word meanings
■ compare different illustrations of the same rhymes
■ visualize characters and settings
■ compose riddles based on nursery rhyme characters.

CROSS-CURRICULAR LINKS

ART AND DESIGN

Draw pictures of nursery rhyme characters.

DRAMA

Mime.

RESOURCES AND CLASSROOM ORGANIZATION

You will need: different Big Book versions of nursery rhymes or a mixture of Big and normal-sized books. *Our Favourite Rhymes* (published by the Longman Book Project) is particularly recommended for its very lively, up-to-date multicultural illustrations. The children could also bring in some of their own nursery rhyme books from home. The children will need drawing materials and copies of photocopiable page 42.

Children work initially as a class and then individually on their illustrations. The photocopiable sheet should be completed individually or in pairs.

WHAT TO DO

Choose any well-known nursery rhyme and read it to the class, discussing the meaning of any difficult or archaic vocabulary (*tuffet, curds and whey, Christmas pie, contrary, night-gown* and so on). Explain that these rhymes are very old and that some of the words in them are not used much nowadays. Now read the same nursery rhyme to the children from several different books and show them the illustrations. What differences can they see in the way the characters look? Why are they different? Explain that different illustrators imagine the same characters in different ways.

Tell the children that they are going to be illustrators themselves now. They are going to draw their own ideas for nursery rhyme characters (such as Miss Muffet, Jack and Jill, the Crooked Man and so on) or scenes with the characters in them (such as Mary Mary's garden or the King's counting house). Make sure the children have plenty of ideas to start them off. Before they begin, ask them to close their eyes and picture in their minds what their characters are wearing, where they are, what they are doing, and so on.

SUGGESTIONS FOR SUPPORT AND EXTENSION

Extend these ideas to answering and making up riddles about nursery rhyme characters. Begin by explaining to the children what riddles are and how they work. Make up some examples for them similar to those on photocopiable page 42. For example, write two short sentences each offering a single clue, with 'Who am I?' as the concluding sentence. The children should then go on to complete the photocopiable sheet, working either on their own, or in pairs for mutual support. Children who succeed in making up their own riddles should be given the opportunity to ask the rest of the class to guess the answers to them.

NOW OR LATER

■ Children's drawings and books could be used to create a 'portrait gallery' display of nursery rhyme characters.
■ Develop the children's ideas of characters and settings by playing 'Mime the rhyme'. Ask individual pupils to take turns to perform simple actions for nursery rhyme characters. For example, *He stuck in his thumb, And pulled out a plum*, while the others try to guess which character they are pretending to be.

WRITING RHYMES

RESOURCES AND CLASSROOM ORGANIZATION

You will need: a Big Book of poetry that shows a simple rhyming pattern and monosyllabic rhyming words. The activity that follows is based on *The Fish Who Could Wish* by John Bush (Oxford University Press). Have a board or flip chart available to write on during the class discussion. The children will then need writing materials and copies of photocopiable page 43 to work on individually.

Children work initially as a class and then individually to complete the photocopiable sheet.

WHAT TO DO

Read the poem to the children several times so that they gain a sense of its rhythm and rhyme scheme. Discuss the content and meaning: children often fail to see that the rhymes in a poem must make sense. Now look at some of the pairs of rhymes

OBJECTIVES

To enable children to:
■ sort rhymes
■ compose rhymes that make sense.

that are used in the poem. Choose children to pick examples, and write them on the board or flip chart. For example:

That silly old fish
Wished he could be
Just like all the other
Fish in the sea.

Now ask the children to pick out the words that rhyme. Underline them. Ask the class to think of other words that rhyme with 'be'. Teach them how to find rhymes by going through the alphabet to try out different onsets. Write down their suggestions ('free', 'tree', 'me', 'tea', 'he', 'key'). *Which of these words could be used in the poem instead of the word 'sea'?* Try substituting them in the context, and establish that none of them would make sense. Repeat this process several times to emphasize that in a rhyming poem the words do not just have to rhyme – they must also fit in with the meaning of the rest of the poem.

Introduce the activity on photocopiable page 43 by explaining to the children that they are now going to write some more titles for poems about unusual animals. When they look for the missing words in the wordbank on the sheet, they will need to find a word that both rhymes and makes sense. They should cross out the words in the wordbank that sound wrong.

SUGGESTIONS FOR SUPPORT AND EXTENSION

A simplified version of the photocopiable sheet could be prepared for less able children by covering over the redundant rhyming words in the wordbank, so that they simply choose the words that rhyme. More able children could go on to compose more rhyming animal poem titles, or write their own poems using one of the titles given on the sheet.

NOW OR LATER

■ Introduce the idea of writing the title for another poem about an animal that can do something unusual. You could start with a cat. *What words rhyme with cat?* List the children's suggestions on the board ('fat', 'that', 'hat', 'bat', 'mat', 'chat', 'rat', 'sat').

■ Now try out each word in a possible title: 'The cat who could…', rejecting those that don't work and underlining those that would make sense in a title.

■ Write the suggested titles that could actually be used for a new poem: 'The cat who could bat' or 'The cat who could chat'.

PERFORMING POETRY

RESOURCES AND CLASSROOM ORGANIZATION

You will need: a Big Book poem that can be divided easily into parts which the children can play and add actions to. The activities that follow specifically refer to

Walking Through the Jungle by Julie Lacombe (Walker Books), together with Brown Bear, Brown Bear, What Do You See? and Polar Bear, Polar Bear, What Do You Hear? both by Bill Martin Jr. (Longman). However, the principles behind these books could be applied to any poems with similar structures. Look for poems which describe a combination of sights, sounds and movements.

Children work initially as a class and are then divided into groups for the role-playing and art work.

OBJECTIVES
To enable children to:
■ memorize patterns and rhymes
■ match movements to words
■ recite poems for an audience.

CROSS-CURRICULAR LINKS
DRAMA
Role-playing.

ART AND DESIGN
Making masks and puppets.

WHAT TO DO

Walking Through the Jungle is a book in which the text and illustrations combine to show the reader the sights and sounds experienced by a little boy as he makes his way through a jungle. The boy meets, in succession, a hissing and wriggling snake, a growling and creeping tiger, a trumpeting, running elephant, a lion roaring and leaping, a monkey chattering and swinging and a crocodile snapping as it wades through the water. Begin by reading the whole poem to the class several times until they can all join in with the sounds that the animals make as you point to them on the page ('Grrrrrr' for the tiger, 'Sssssss' for the snake, and so on). Now focus on the actions that are shown in the pictures, pointing out the words that describe these ('creeping', 'leaping', 'swinging', and so on). Ask individual children to come out in front of the class and perform the actions that match each word.

Now divide the class into six groups; one to play the part of each animal by miming its actions and making the appropriate sounds. Choose individual children to act as narrators and recite the relevant text, or ask the whole class to provide the narration in chorus, for example:

Tigers' group: 'Creeping through the jungle, what do you see?'
(Mime creeping)
'Grrrrrr!'
Narrator: 'I can see a tiger, looking at me.'

Brown Bear, Brown Bear and *Polar Bear, Polar Bear* could be dramatized in exactly the same way. Both poems have a similar structure and are also concerned with the sights and sounds of different animals:

Polar Bear, Polar Bear, what do you hear?
I hear a lion, roaring in my ear

NOW OR LATER

■ The children's actions and recitation could be practised and polished for a performance as a whole class.
■ Children could make animal masks and tails and wear the appropriate colours for their particular 'character'. *Polar Bear, Polar Bear* contains illustrations of children wearing animal outfits that you could use as a source of inspiration.
■ Alternatively, each group could make stick or glove puppet versions of their particular animal and perform its actions with their puppets.

MAKING A RHYMING DICTIONARY

OBJECTIVES

To enable children to:
■ compose simple rhymes
■ use alphabetical order.

RESOURCES AND CLASSROOM ORGANIZATION

You will need: some alphabet Big Books or alphabet friezes or posters to look at with the children. Copies of simple dictionaries should also be available. It would be useful, though not essential, to have a copy of *A Simple Rhyming Dictionary* Big Book (published by Longman Pelican). Have a board or flip chart ready on which to model the activity for the class.

To start the children off with the writing activity, you will need to prepare 26 A4 sheets or cards with each letter of the alphabet, plus the following headings: an, bat, cap, dig, end, fog, got, how, in, jam, king, lit, men, night, old, play, quick, run, see, take, us, vet, will, your, zoo. The 'x' card will not be used, but should be included. Write 'extra page' on it. More able pairs of children can be given more than one card to tackle. The children will need pencils and/or crayons. Completed cards should be punched and kept in a clip file.

Introduce the activity with the children working as a class, then divide them into pairs to work on separate dictionary entries. Finally, the class should be brought together again to sort the entries into alphabetical order.

WHAT TO DO

Revise the order of the alphabet with the children by looking at Big Book alphabets and display posters. Play alphabet games where the children sit in a circle and each child is assigned a letter in alphabetical order and has to think of a word that begins with that letter.

Show the children some simple dictionaries and discuss what they are for (to tell us what words mean). Ask the children how they know where to look for a particular word in a dictionary. Make sure that everyone understands that the words are arranged in alphabetical order.

Now go on to explain that not all dictionaries give word meanings. Some dictionaries give information about other things that people want to know. For example, if you wanted to think of some rhymes to use in a poem, you might use a rhyming dictionary. Show the class how to look up words in a rhyming dictionary if you have one available. Otherwise demonstrate on the board or flip chart how the entries are organized in alphabetical order and brainstorm some examples of entries and rhymes for words beginning with A, B, C and so on.

Then divide the children into pairs and give each pair one of the alphabet cards or sheets that you prepared earlier. Explain that they now have to make a list of words that rhyme with the word at the top of their card. This could be done initially as a rough draft, or they could write straight on to the card.

When all the entries are complete, reassemble the children as a class and sort the entries into alphabetical order with them. This could be done physically by arranging the children into a line or circle. Collect the cards in order and put them into a clip file labelled 'Our Rhyming Dictionary' to be kept as a resource in the book corner.

NOW OR LATER

■ Children could illustrate some of the words that they have listed. Further entries could be added to the file. The lists of rhyming words under each heading could be organized into alphabetical order.

Ready to go! IDEAS FOR BIG BOOKS

The zoo concert

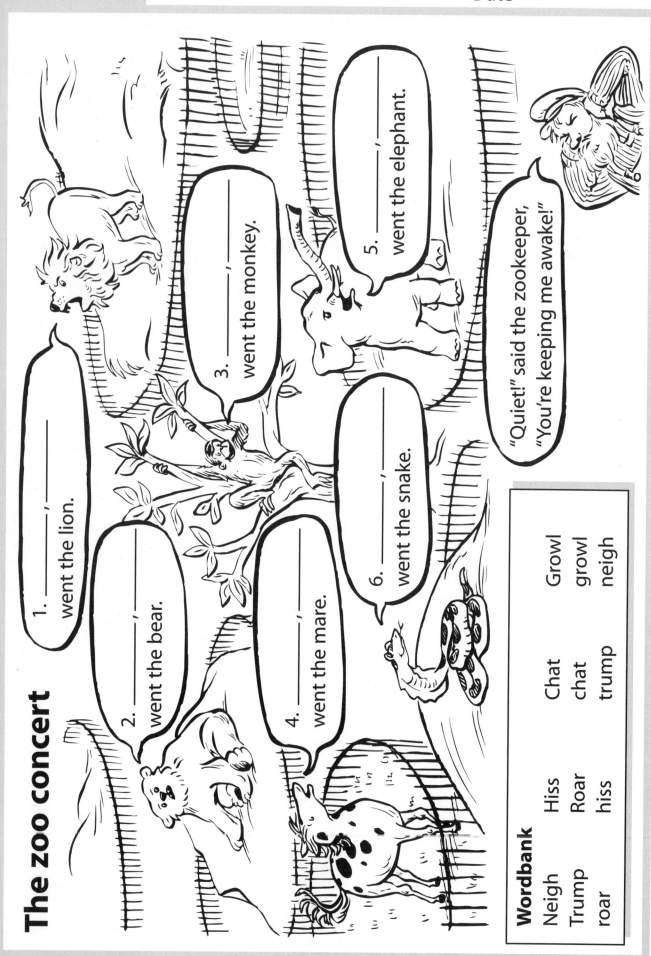

1. _____, _____ went the lion.

2. _____, _____ went the bear.

3. _____, _____ went the monkey.

4. _____, _____ went the mare.

5. _____, _____ went the elephant.

6. _____, _____ went the snake.

"Quiet!" said the zookeeper,
"You're keeping me awake!"

Wordbank

Neigh	Hiss	Growl
Trump	Roar	growl
roar	hiss	neigh
	Chat	
	chat	
	trump	

Photocopiables

40

Guess the rhyme

What can you see?

A bird in a _____

What do you like?

A ride on my _____

What can you make?

A butterfly _____

What can you do?

I can tie up my _____

What can you say?

I am going out to _____

                     OK!

■   Now make some lists of rhymes.

see	like	make	do	say
_____	_____	_____	_____	_____
_____	_____	_____	_____	_____
_____	_____	_____	_____	_____

Ready to go! IDEAS FOR BIG BOOKS

Nursery rhyme riddles

Both my names begin with M.
I don't like spiders.
Who am I?

_____

I fell down a hill.
My brother is called Jack.
Who am I?

_____

I fell off a wall.
I am shaped like an egg.
Who am I?

_____

My name begins with J.
I am a good boy.
Who am I?

_____

■ Now make up your own riddles on the back of the sheet.

Ready to go! IDEAS FOR BIG BOOKS

Unusual animals

Which word fits where?

The fish who could _____

The cow who could _____

The rat who could _____

The pig who could _____

The sheep who could _____

The goat who could _____

The fox who could _____

The dog who could _____

The bear who could _____

Wordbank

dig	jog	big
box	chair	chat
coat	bow	dish
fog	weep	stare
float	sat	deep
now	wish	rocks

Using a variety of types of Big Book information texts, the following activities aim to help children to:
- distinguish between fiction and non-fiction
- use contents lists and indexes to find specific information
- identify key words and prepare for note-making
- ask their own questions and search for answers
- read, summarize and record information
- understand the purpose of captions and labels
- know how to write a set of instructions
- make their own simple information books.

WHAT IS AN INFORMATION BOOK?

OBJECTIVES

To enable children to:
- compare typical features of fiction and information texts
- recognize examples of each type of text
- understand that information texts are not read in the same way as fiction.

RESOURCES AND CLASSROOM ORGANIZATION

You will need: at least one Big Book fiction text (a short and simple traditional tale that begins 'Once upon a time' would be ideal) and at least one Big Book information text. The latter should contain numbered pages, a list of contents, an index, captioned pictures and labelled drawings and diagrams. A glossary or 'helpful words' section would also be useful. Not all non-fiction Big Books have these features, but you will find them in *Magic Beans* and *Discovery World* titles (both published by Heinemann) and in *Factfinders* (in *Oxford Reading Tree*, published by Oxford University Press). If possible, choose fiction and information texts with linked themes, for example *The Three Little Pigs* (*Literacy Links*, published by Mimosa Publications) and *Building a House* (*Oxford Reading Tree*). Have a board or flip chart available on which to note the children's responses during the discussion that follows the Big Book reading.

Children work initially as a class, then in groups of four to six, to sort books and finally complete the photocopiable sheet in mixed-ability pairs. For the sorting activity each group should be given a selection of normal-sized fiction and non-fiction books (three or more of each type), and each pair will need pencils and a copy of photocopiable page 57.

WHAT TO DO

Read the fiction text to the children. Then ask them what kind of book they think it is. Write their suggestions on the board or chart (for example, 'it is a Big Book', '...a story book', '...a fairy tale') and ask them how they know this. ('It starts with *Once upon a time*', 'It isn't true', 'It's make-believe', 'It has a beginning, a middle and an ending'.)

Now compare the fiction book with a non-fiction text, preferably one with a linked theme. Point out the common theme, if there is one – 'This is also a book about building a house'. Then show the children the relevant pages, noting down the distinguishing features of a non-fiction book as you do so. Ask the children how the information book is different from the story book. Discuss the cover. What do they think the book will have inside? How might it begin? Show the children the list of contents. *What is this for?* Explain that with this type of book, it is not necessary to read all the pages from the beginning to the end as you would read a story. You use it to help you find out something that you want to know.

Refer to one of the items in the contents list. *What page would you turn to if you wanted to find out something about…? Where else in the book could you look to find more information about a particular subject?* Show the children the index and talk about how to use it. Look up some references that the children suggest and read the relevant information to the class. Point out any diagrams, labels and captions, making sure that the children understand the terminology. Explain how all these elements provide extra information and also make the information clearer for the reader. If the book has a glossary explain what this is and show the children how it is used to explain what difficult words mean.

Go back and summarize the differences between the two types of book. Show the class more examples of each type if it seems appropriate.

Tell the children that they are now going to sort some books into fiction and non-fiction categories. They should work in groups, look at the books, talk about them together and put them into two piles. When they have done this, each group should show the rest of the class which book they have chosen to put where, and be prepared to explain their reasons for doing so.

NOW OR LATER

■ Children should now have some understanding of the distinguishing features of fiction and non-fiction books. They could now go on to sort different pieces of writing and decide which type of book they would fit into. Read out some extracts from the Big Books, or from the books that they have sorted, to give them an idea of what they will have to do.

■ Finally, children should complete photocopiable page 57, working in pairs of mixed ability for support.

USING A CONTENTS PAGE AND INDEX

OBJECTIVES

To enable children to:
■ understand the purpose of contents pages and indexes
■ scan them effectively.

RESOURCES AND CLASSROOM ORGANIZATION

You will need: an information Big Book linked to a topic that the class is currently studying. Make sure that its contents list and index are well thought out and helpful to the reader. The example specifically referred to in this activity is *Building a House* by Valerie Fawcett in the *Factfinders* series (from *Oxford Reading Tree*, published by Oxford University Press).

Using the index as a guide, prepare some large cards with key words that you are going to ask the class to look up. Check that the children will be able to relate some of the words to the contents list.

Children work with the Big Book as a whole class to complete this activity.

WHAT TO DO

Show the class the cover of the Big Book that you have chosen. What sort of information would they expect it to contain? Show them the contents page (make the link between the words 'contents' and 'contain') and compare their predictions with the actual list. Discuss the purpose of the contents page, and explain how it gives a general guide to what the book is about and where to look for information about different subjects. Explain to the children that often a quick look at the contents page of any book will be enough to tell them whether it is likely to contain the information that they want to find.

Now give out the key word cards to individual children and ask them to hold them up in front of the class. Explain that, for example, you want to find out about pipes, using the *Building a House* book, and ask the child holding the card to read out the word. Point to the contents page and ask the rest of the children where you might be able to find the information that you want. Choose a child to come to the front, point out and read aloud the item in the contents list that they have identified. In *Building a House* this could be (if identified correctly) either 'The drain' on page 10 or 'Water and heating' on page 18 . Ask the child to turn to the relevant pages. Show the children how to scan the pages on this topic quickly to find the word that is written on the card. Ask individual children to point to the word and read the sentences around it. Could they be sure of finding the word 'pipes' on these pages? What if it hadn't been there? How could they find out for sure, without reading the whole book, whether it contained any information about pipes?

Show the children the index and explain that this is a list of the most important topics and names in the book and the pages on which information about them can be found. Talk about how the words are arranged in alphabetical order like those in a dictionary so that they can be looked up quickly. *Who has found the word 'pipes'? What pages does it say that the word is on?* (Pages 10–11, and pages 18–19). Demonstrate that they are the same pages that the contents page had listed.

NOW OR LATER

■ Repeat the process using the other word cards that you have prepared.
■ Finally, discuss with the children whether they found using the index or the contents page a more helpful way of accessing information.

FINDING WHAT MATTERS

RESOURCES AND CLASSROOM ORGANIZATION

You will need: a Big Book with a health or safety theme and some information posters that endorse the theme. This activity is based on the Big Book *Look Out on the Road* (in the *Rainbows* series published by Evans). The text uses a mixture of speech bubbles and narrative and concerns a family that goes out shopping and then goes for a country walk. The text also offers general advice and information which is addressed to the reader. The illustrations are a mixture of coloured drawings and photographs. Have a board or flip chart available on which to write the safety rules that the children identify. Each child will need a copy of photocopiable page 58, a pencil and coloured crayons.

Children work initially as a class with the Big Book and then individually to complete the photocopiable sheet. The final work on poster design could be done collaboratively in pairs.

WHAT TO DO

Begin by reading the Big Book with the children so that they have an overview of how it works. Now focus on a particular health or safety issue that you want the class to draw out of the text. For example if you use *Look Out on the Road*, tell the children that you want them to pick out words that are about how to keep safe on the road and then to help you to make a list of rules for road safety. Point to the speech bubbles. *What are the people in the pictures saying to one another? Which speeches are about how to be safe?* (*I must wear a seat belt…*). *Which are not?* (*We are in the car.*) *Look at the pictures. What do they show about how to be safe?* (Parents fastening seat belts for the children.) Ask the children to express this as a safety rule in their own words and write the rule on the board or chart.

> ## Safety Rules
> 1. Wear a seat belt in the car.
> 2. Don't cross the road when the red man is showing.
> 3. ....

Look for other rules contained in the speech bubbles and write them in the same way. Now help the class to look for safety advice in the rest of the text ('The red man shows us that it's not safe to cross the road'), sorting out which sentences are relevant and which are not, and noting down any new rules as before. When you have noted down all the rules that the book mentions, read the list back with the children.

Explain that posters are a quick way for people to read warnings or rules about health and safety. Show them some examples if available. Tell the children that they are now going to colour in a poster about using a pelican crossing. (Make sure that the children understand what a pelican crossing is and how it works.) It will be very important to use the right colours for the men on the signals. Give the children the poster on photocopiable page 58 to complete.

NOW OR LATER

■ Discuss the posters that the children have coloured in. Point out that the information on a poster should be clear and simple so that people notice it and understand it easily.

■ Refer the children back to the list of rules that they made when they read the safety advice in the book. Working in pairs for mutual support, they should now choose one of the rules from the list and make their own poster about it. The poster should have simple drawings and a short, clear message.

OBJECTIVES

To enable children to:
■ process information
■ focus attention on key illustrations, words and phrases
■ prepare children for note-making.

CROSS-CURRICULAR LINKS

ART AND DESIGN
Making road safety or health education posters.

WHAT DO WE WANT TO KNOW?

OBJECTIVES
To enable children to:
■ generate questions
■ locate and record answers.

RESOURCES AND CLASSROOM ORGANIZATION

You will need: an information Big Book which is linked to a topic that the class is studying. It should have a contents list and an index. Prepare a board or flip chart with the same headings as photocopiable page 59, on which to record each stage of the process of asking and answering questions with the whole class. Later the children will use photocopiable page 59 as a writing frame to help them to repeat the process in small groups. For this part of the activity each group will need a selection of information books (not necessarily Big Books) to share. Ideally these should contain contents and index pages.

WHAT TO DO

Show the class the cover of the Big Book and read out the title with them. Ask the children what they know about the subject already, and write their responses on the board. Now ask them what they would like to find out about the subject. Record their replies in the form of questions. Refer back to the Big Book. Which of their questions do they think the book might have the answers to? How are they going to find out? Will they need to read the whole book? Model with the class how to use the contents and index pages to locate specific information (refer to the activity 'Using a contents page and index' on page 46). Then ask individual children to come out and find the relevant words in the Big Book.

Ask the children to compose sentences about the facts that they have discovered, and write these down for all to see. Did the book have the answers to all their questions? If not, where could they look to find out more? (Other information books, encyclopaedias, CD ROMs and so on.) Explain that some questions may be very difficult or even impossible to answer.

NOW OR LATER

■ Taking the same topic, or a new one, the children should now go on in their groups to use other information books in the same way: pooling the knowledge that they have already and recording their questions and discoveries on photocopiable page 59.

■ Each group could present their work orally to the rest of the class, or go on to make a large illustrated poster on their topic to be displayed in the classroom.

CONCEPT MAPPING

RESOURCES AND CLASSROOM ORGANIZATION

You will need: a non-fiction Big Book with a lively mix of information on a topic that the class is studying. For this activity it is preferable that the book should not feature contents and index pages. Recommended titles include *A Seed in Need* or *The Drop Goes Plop* by Sam Godwin (in *MY Bees* series published by Macdonald) both are colourful, cartoon-style picture books with speech bubbles, diagrams and unconventionally presented explanatory text, or *Splish, Splash, Splosh!* a book about water in the *Wonderwise* series (published by Franklin Watts), another lively picture book packed with information about different aspects of water. Have a board or flip chart ready, together with a selection of different coloured markers.

Children work as a the class to complete this activity while you record and model the concept mapping process. You will need to identify the various strands of information to be mapped out before embarking on the modelling process with the children.

WHAT TO DO

Read the Big Book through several times with the class, discussing the contents thoroughly and giving the children plenty of opportunities to raise any questions, concerns and misunderstandings.

Then ask the children to explain in their own words what they have learned about the topic (of water, for example) from the book. Refer back to the book to check or confirm the information if necessary. Using a spider diagram centred around the general topic, map out the facts that are identified by the class.

Now ask the children to group the different facts around the diagram into items that go together. For example, which facts are about the sea? Point to those that the children identify and re-read them. Discuss whether they really are about the sea. Once everyone is agreed on this, tell the class that you are going to show that they are about the sea by underlining them in blue. Make a key by writing the word 'Sea' in blue in a corner of the paper. Repeat this process with other items around the diagram (for example, grouping them under the headings 'Rain', 'What happens to dirty water' and 'What we use water for at home'), using a different colour to show which information belongs under which heading.

Sea water makes waves	Rain can make floods	Boats sail on the sea	We use water to wash up
We use water for the shower	**Water**		Rain comes from clouds
Dolphins live in the sea	Dirty water goes down the drain	You can get rainbows when it rains	We use water to flush the toilet

When all the facts have been sorted under the appropriate headings, display each group together, either by rewriting each set of facts as a list under its heading, or by cutting out and rearranging the items from the original brainstorming sheet.

NOW OR LATER

■ Children could use this method of concept mapping to organize information collected from other books, or from a combination of sources such as television programmes, CD ROMs, posters, books and word of mouth.

■ The process could also be used in brainstorming 'What we already know' and 'What we want to find out', with different groups of children looking up information under the various headings that are generated (see the activity 'What do we want to know?' opposite).

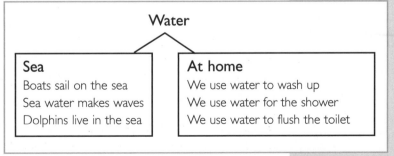

Water

Sea	At home
Boats sail on the sea	We use water to wash up
Sea water makes waves	We use water for the shower
Dolphins live in the sea	We use water to flush the toilet

OBJECTIVES
To enable children to:
■ summarize information
■ see how facts can be grouped together
■ make and use a simple key
■ begin to understand some of the different ways in which information texts can be organized.

49

READING AND EXTRACTING INFORMATION

OBJECTIVES

To enable children to:
■ read and remember facts
■ recount information orally
■ develop confidence in speaking
■ listen to others when it is their turn to speak.

RESOURCES AND CLASSROOM ORGANIZATION

You will need: a Big Book, with a contents list, on a subject which can easily be divided into four to six sub-topics for example *Seasons* from the *Discovery World* series (published by Heinemann) or *Senses* from the *Body Works* series (published by Belitha Books) *or All Kinds of Families* from the *Oxford Reading Tree* (published by Oxford University Press – which describes six different neighbouring families).

For this activity you should read the Big Book with one group of children at a time. You will need to organize the class into as many groups as you have sub-topics. The children begin by working with you to become 'experts' in their sub-topic groups, and then move into new groups to share their knowledge individually with the children who have found out about the other sub-topics.

Assign to each child in the class the number or name of their sub-topic (for example 1, 2, 3, 4 or spring, summer, autumn, winter) and begin by reading the Big Book with all the 1s (or the 'spring' group). While you do this the rest of the class should work independently, preparing for their presentation by making notes or drawing illustrations related to the topic.

WHAT TO DO

Explain to the group that you are going to read some of the information in the Big Book with them and that they are then going to split up and tell the children in the

other groups what they have found out. Select the pages that you are going to read, first asking the children to identify them by using the contents list or the index to look for the word for their particular subject.

Read the information with them and discuss the pictures. Then question the group to make sure that they have assimilated the information. Now tell the children that you are going to give them a few more minutes to look at the page. Then you are going to close the book and ask them to tell one another what they can remember about it.

Give each child in turn the opportunity to recount the information to the rest of the group, supporting individuals where necessary. Do not allow any other member of the group to interrupt. When all of the first group have become 'experts' in their subject, they should go on to independent work. Repeat this procedure with the rest of the groups until each of them have become 'experts'.

The children should now be regrouped so that there is a full range of 'experts' in each set (for example, seven groups of four in a class of twenty-eight). If the numbers do not work out exactly, put two experts on the same subject into some groups.

The final stage of the activity is to fit the final 'pieces of the jigsaw' together by having each of the 'experts' in turn share their knowledge with the rest of the group (for example, no. 1 tells nos. 2, 3 and 4 about spring; No. 2 tells 1, 3 and 4 about summer and so on).

SUGGESTIONS FOR SUPPORT AND EXTENSION

The children could be supported by working to develop their 'expertise' in pairs. Older children or independent readers could become experts through independent reading without the intervention of the teacher.

NOW OR LATER

This activity could also be used with fiction texts, by dividing a story into episodes or chapters for the children to recount.

USING CAPTIONS AND LABELS

OBJECTIVES

To enable children to:
■ understand the function of captions
■ use labels as a way of recording information.

CROSS-CURRICULAR LINKS
ART
Drawing pictures and diagrams.

RESOURCES AND CLASSROOM ORGANIZATION

You will need: a Big Book which contains both captions and labelled drawings or diagrams. For younger children an ideal example would be *My Body* in the *Discovery World* series (published by Heinemann), in which each double-page spread consists of a captioned photograph of a child pointing to a part of the body ('This is my head') opposite a labelled close-up, or X-ray, showing the names for each feature (nose, eye, mouth, ear and so on).

Have some Post-it notes ready to cover up some of the captions in the book. You will also need a board or flip chart on which to sketch a copy of one of the labelled drawings or diagrams, and a cut out set of labels and some Blu-Tack to go with it. Each child will need scissors, glue and a copy of photocopiable page 60. For the extension activities they will need drawing and writing materials.

Children begin this activity by working as a class with the Big Book and then discuss your sketched diagram. They then work individually to complete the photocopiable sheet.

WHAT TO DO

Before looking at the structural features of the book, read the text and discuss the pictures thoroughly with the whole class so that they have a general idea of its content and meaning. Then use the Post-it notes to cover up some of the captions towards the end of the book. When you have done this, re-read the book to the class, pointing out that some of the pictures have writing with them which tells the reader what the pictures are about. Explain that these bits of writing are called captions. Words explaining what pictures are about are also used in displays. Can the children point to any captions that go with the pictures on the walls of the classroom?

We painted portraits of each other.

Joe by Jack   Jack by Joe   Chlöe by Izzy   Izzy by Chlöe

Ask the children to identify some of the captions in the Big Book. When they have identified several captions correctly, move on to those that you have covered over. What words do the children think should be written on the Post-it notes? Write out their suggestions and then remove the cards and compare them with the actual captions. Were they right? If not, did their suggestions make sense?

Tell the children that another way of writing about pictures and diagrams is to put labels on them to point out the names of different parts. Refer to the book to illustrate how labels can be used. Finally, show the children your own sketch or diagram. Hold up the labels that you have made, one by one, and ask individual children to fix them onto the sketch with Blu-Tack. Draw lines to make the links more specific if you need to.

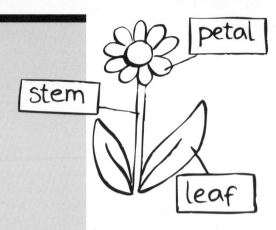

Now or later

■ Give each child a copy of photocopiable page 60. Ask them to label the drawing by cutting out the words and sticking them in place. They can draw lines to show exactly which part of the body the label refers to.

■ If the children are confident about doing this, they could go on to make their own captions and labels for topic-related drawings and diagrams to be displayed in the classroom or collected together and made into books for the class library.

Writing instructions

Objectives

To enable children to:
■ sequence a procedure step-by-step
■ use the imperative voice
■ make drawings or diagrams to explain things.

Cross-curricular links

Art and design

Plan a layout and draw diagrams for instructions. Design and illustrate birthday cards.

Design and technology

Making puppets.

Resources and classroom organization

You will need: a Big Book which sets out clearly organized instructions for making something, such as *Making Puppets* in the *Magic Bean* series (published by Heinemann). Decide on an article from the book that the children will make, and prepare any materials that they will need to be able to do this. For the practical parts of this activity the children will work individually. During subsequent discussions about how to produce a set of instructions they will work as a whole class.

When the children go on to make birthday cards, they will need some card, pencils, scissors and coloured crayons. Finally, each child will need a copy of the writing frame on photocopiable page 61.

What to do

Start by reading aloud the set of instructions that you have decided to use. Have the necessary materials laid out ready for the children. Then read out and discuss what they are instructed to do step-by-step, making sure that each child is clear about the procedures. Leave the Big Book open where everyone can see it, and help the children to follow the instructions and make the article – showing them what to do at each stage 'Blue Peter' style if necessary.

When the puppets or whatever are made, refer back to the Big Book and discuss the form that the instructions take with the class – a list of 'What you will need', followed by a sequence of numbered instructions, with diagrams to provide visual support. Check the children have understood the idea of using the imperative to write instructions by giving examples of inappropriate language and asking whether they sound right. For example, 'First I drew the pattern and then I cut out the shape.' 'If I were you I would get a pencil and some paper ready, then...' both sound wrong. Instructions should tell the reader what to do.

NOW OR LATER

■ How helpful did the children find the set of instructions that they have just used? Was anything missed out that should have been written down? Was everything explained clearly? Tell the children that they are now going to explain how to make something themselves. Their instructions will be used by another class, so they will have to be very clear.

■ First of all, they are going to make something themselves – a birthday card. Then they are going to write their instructions for making it.

Give out the materials. Show the sample cards, discussing design possibilities and appropriate wording, and then set the children to design and make their own cards, supporting them with ideas and suggestions as necessary.

When the cards have been made, ask each child to make a set of instructions, referring back to the format seen in the Big Book, and using photocopiable page 61 as a first draft. The instructions should then be evaluated, amended and redrafted if necessary, before they are passed over to another class and put to the test.

BUILDING A WORDBANK

RESOURCES AND CLASSROOM ORGANIZATION

You will need: an information Big Book that could be used as a source for topic-related words. The ideal Big Book to use for starting off this activity is *Our Five Senses* in the *Factfinders* series from the *Oxford Reading Tree* (published by Oxford University Press). This book contains some excellent examples of wordbanks in its sections on 'Touch' ('How things feel to me: smooth, prickly, warm, cold') and 'Taste' ('Things I like to taste: honey, chips, sausages, bananas, oranges'). If this book is not available, you could make a simple topic-related wordlist to show to the class. Prepare a board or flip chart with a suitable heading for your wordbank to be used in the class discussion. Each child should have a copy of photocopiable page 62 and coloured crayons and writing materials should be available.

Children begin the activity by working as a class and then continue in mixed ability pairs to complete the photocopiable sheet.

WHAT TO DO

Ask the children if they know what a bank is. Explain that it is a place where people put their money to keep it safe until they want to use it. Do they know what a wordbank is? Talk about keeping words together in a safe place until you want to use them. Tell the children that they are going to collect together some words about a topic that you have chosen, and write them down to be used later. Show the class an example of what you mean, using the wordbanks shown in *Our Five Senses* if it is available. Discuss why wordbanks like these might be useful displayed on the classroom wall (so that children can read them, remember the words, spell them correctly when they write them).

Now read an appropriate Big Book and ask the children to pick out the words related to your chosen topic. If you are looking at pictures, it might be a topic such as 'clothes' or 'colours'. If you are looking for specific words, it might be names of 'minibeasts' or 'foods' or 'parts of the body'. In this case ask individual children to

OBJECTIVES
To enable children to:
■ widen their vocabulary
■ collect topic-related words
■ classify words.

come out, point to and read out the words that they identify. Write the word in the wordbank and ask the whole class to read it again. Make sure that all the children understand what the word means.

When the wordbank has exhausted the possibilities of the book that you are using, re-read the whole set of words with the class.

NOW OR LATER

■ Distribute copies of photocopiable page 62 and read out the words to the class if necessary. Children have to sort the words and put them into the appropriate wordbank. The words could be copied or cut out and stuck in place according to the age and ability of the children.

When the words are in place, children can colour around the colour words and illustrate the clothes words.

This type of sorting activity could be used to help the children to classify other topic-related words.

■ Big Books could be word-searched in a similar way for phonics activities (for example, 'banking' all the words beginning with a particular letter), or grammar work (for example, looking for proper nouns or adjectives).

Once children have understood the idea they could work independently, collecting and classifying words from normal-sized books.

MAKING AN ANIMAL FACT FILE

OBJECTIVES

To enable children to:
■ locate information
■ organize facts
■ record and illustrate what they have found out.

CROSS-CURRICULAR LINKS

ART

Drawing animals.

SCIENCE

Animal adaptation.

RESOURCES AND CLASSROOM ORGANIZATION

You will need: an information Big Book or books containing several different snippets of easily categorized information about animals. *The Minibeast Encyclopaedia* in *the Discovery World* series (published by Heinemann) would be ideal. In this book each page entry offers a mixture of pictorial and written information about the appearance, size, habitat and feeding habits of each particular creature, without explicitly using subheadings or captions naming these features. The entries are also in alphabetical order.

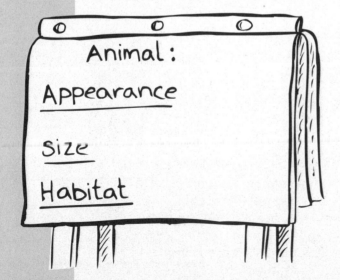

Prepare a board or flip chart with the general heading 'Animal', followed by the subheadings listed above. Children work initially as a class and then complete photocopiable page 63 working in pairs or small groups of mixed ability. Each pair or group will need at least one information book about animals to share.

WHAT TO DO

Read about a particular animal with the children, locating the relevant page by using the index or alphabet (if using *The Minibeast Encyclopaedia*) if possible. Refer to the board or flip chart and explain to the class what each heading means. Then ask which information from the book belongs under which heading. Write the correct answers on the board, using note form rather than complete sentences, for example:

(under 'Wasp') **Feeding**
    Eats fruit and sweet things.

Make some quick sketches to illustrate each written note.
    Repeat the exercise of reading and processing information for other animals if necessary, until most of the children have understood the idea of sorting relevant facts and writing them down in note form. The children should then go on to compile their own animal fact files using photocopiable page 63 as a framework for writing and drawing.

NOW OR LATER

■ Discuss the links between animal habitats and feeding habits. Ask the children to think about whether the animal's appearance protects it in any way, for example by providing camouflage.
■ Share the completed fact files by mounting them on the classroom wall for everyone to read or by collecting them together back-to-back in an A4 display file to make a book for the class library.

MAKING A COUNTING OR ALPHABET BOOK

RESOURCES AND CLASSROOM ORGANIZATION

You will need: simple alphabet and counting Big Books to use as models. Have a board or flip chart ready on which to write down ideas. Write the alphabet or the numbers that you wish to use in large print across the top. The children will need pencils and colouring crayons, together with large sheets of card or thick paper for their book pages. If they are to cut out the illustrations, you will need to prepare a set of simple drawings and provide scissors and glue.

To produce the alphabet book, the children could work either individually or in pairs to make their pages. For the counting book, younger children should work in twos or threes to help each other with the illustrations. Older infants could work on their own. Before work begins decide who is going to make the page for each number or letter.

WHAT TO DO

If the children are making an alphabet book, read the Big Book that you have chosen as a model and discuss how it is constructed: with the large letters on the pages set out in

OBJECTIVES
To enable children to:
■ know initial letters
■ match objects to numbers
■ sequence numbers and letters
■ copy the format and layout of a simple book.

CROSS-CURRICULAR LINKS
MATHS
Developing concepts of number and order.

ART
Making illustrations.

alphabetical order and the illustrations showing objects whose initial letters match the one printed on the page. Explain to the class that they are going to make their own alphabet book, and ask for suggestions for objects that they could draw

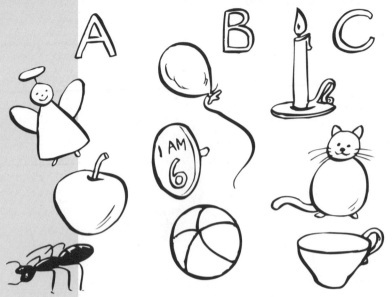

beginning with the letter A. They should choose something plain and simple. Note down suitable ideas on the board, and repeat for the letters B and C.

Divide the children into appropriate groups and tell each group which letter it is to be responsible for. The children should print the letter on their page so that it is large and clear, and then draw objects that begin with that letter. If they are stuck for ideas they could ask for help or look at an illustrated dictionary. Give out the writing and drawing materials, and offer help where necessary.

If the children are making a counting book proceed in a similar way, by first looking at how the model Big Book works, then asking for suggestions for illustrations, and finally setting up the task.

SUGGESTIONS FOR SUPPORT AND EXTENSION
For the alphabet book
■ To introduce the activity, younger or less able children could be given separate objects or pictures to match with plastic letters. To make their pages they could draw the objects or cut out the pictures, and draw around the corresponding letters.
■ Older or more able children could write the words for the objects that they draw. They could try making a themed alphabet about a particular subject, for example animals, children's names or food.
For the counting book
■ Younger children could be given counters or other objects to match with a plastic number or one that is written on card. When they have put out the correct number of counters they could copy the number and draw the counters or other objects on their page.

■ To extend the activity the sequence of numbers could run in units up to ten, twenty, or thirty. The counting itself could be done in 2s, 5s, 10s, and so on. The sequence of numbers could go up, down or both.

NOW OR LATER
■ Children could help you to assemble the pages and put them in the correct order. Use a ring binder, a hole punch and treasury tags, a spiral binder or a slide binder to fix them together. Alternatively, tape the pages at the sides to make a zigzag book.
■ Hold a competition for the best jacket design.

Put the books in the boxes

■ Choose whether each piece of text should go in the fiction or non-fiction box.

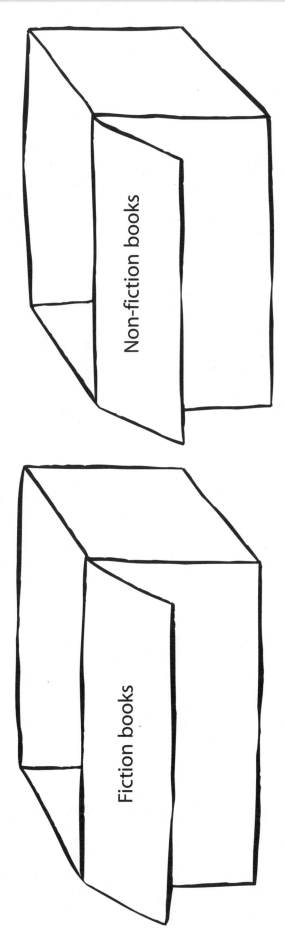

Non-fiction books

Fiction books

Once upon a time there were three bears.

All of a sudden the giant woke up.

"I don't want to go to bed yet," said Tom.

Cut out two pieces of felt.

Summer is the season that comes after spring.

The pipes in the house are joined to a drain.

Photocopiables

Using a pelican crossing

When you see this sign

DO NOT
CROSS
THE ROAD.

It is safe to
cross now.

But LOOK and LISTEN to make sure.

Finding facts

Subject _____

What we already know _____

_____

_____

_____

_____

What we want to find out _____

_____

_____

_____

_____

What we have found out _____

_____

_____

_____

_____

Photocopiables

Parts of the body

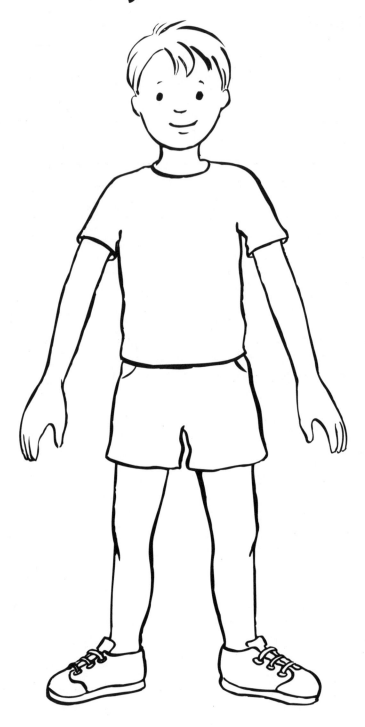

■ Use these words to label the drawing:

head	leg	neck	foot
arm	chest	hand	shoulder

Ready to go! **IDEAS FOR BIG BOOKS**

Photocopiables

How to make a birthday card

What you will need

_____

_____

_____

What to do

1.	First
2.	Next
3.	Then
4.	

■ Write on the back of the sheet if you need to.

Colours and clothes

■ Sort these words into the correct wordbanks:

red	coat	yellow	hat
sock	blue	green	shirt
trousers	orange	black	shorts
skirt	pink	jumper	brown

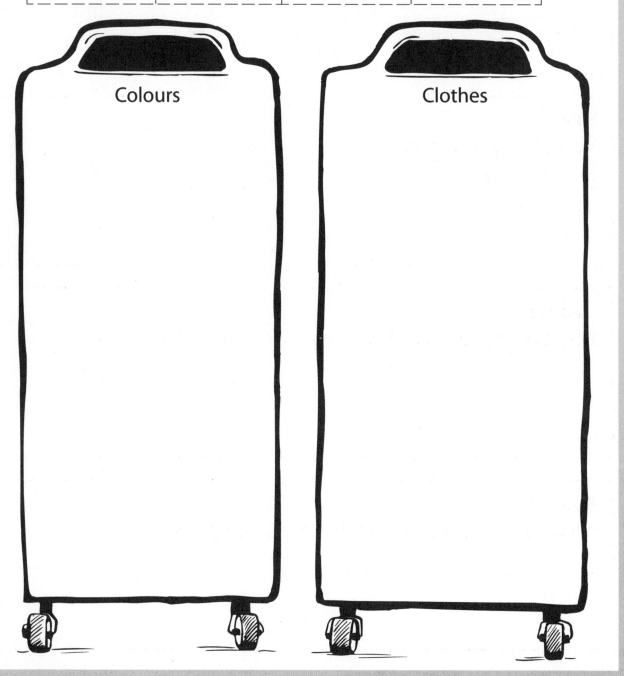

Colours   Clothes

Ready to go! IDEAS FOR BIG BOOKS

The Photocopiables

Name   Date

My animal fact file

Animal _____

Appearance
What does your animal look like?

Size
How big is your animal?

Habitat
Where does your animal live? How does it make its home?

Feeding
What does your animal eat? How does it get food?

Ready to go! IDEAS FOR BIG BOOKS

NATIONAL STANDARDS FOR KEY SKILLS

All of the ideas listed are designed to develop children's reading ability and knowledge of words. Other key literacy skills focused on in each activity are summarized below.

Title	Key skills
Section 1	
Understanding cover information	Understanding terminology about books. Predicting.
What comes next?	Predicting.
Observing basic punctuation	Using full stops, question marks and exclamation marks.
Working with sentences	Identifying, making and punctuating sentences.
Sequencing events	Observing chronological order.
Finding the plot	Plotting key events on a storyboard.
Who's who?	Recognizing and describing story characters.
Who says what?	Reading speech, role-play and performance.
Reading the pictures	Using initial letter sounds and positional language.
Setting the scene	Developing an understanding of story settings.
Changing the story	Using a known story as a model for a new version.
Retelling aloud	Memorizing. Developing confidence in speaking.
Reviewing the story	Expressing opinions. Reasoning.
Section 2	
A book of similes	Making comparisons. Using poetic language.
Orchestrating rhythm	Identifying syllables and patterns of rhythm.
Recognizing rhyme	Identifying and creating rhymes.
Working with nursery rhymes	Recognizing characters. Composing riddles.
Writing rhymes	Composing rhymes that make sense.
Performing poetry	Memorizing, reciting and dramatising.
Making a rhyming dictionary	Composing rhymes. Using alphabetical order.
Section 3	
What is an information book?	Comparing fiction and information texts.
Using a contents page and index	Scanning for information. Using alphabetical order.
Finding what matters	Locating and processing information.
What do we want to know?	Asking questions and looking up answers.
Concept mapping	Summarizing and sorting information.
Reading and extracting information	Memorizing facts. Sharing information orally.
Using captions and labels	Understanding function of captions. Labelling.
Writing instructions	Sequencing a procedure. Using imperative voice.
Building a wordbank	Collecting and classifying topic-related words.
Making an animal fact file	Locating, organizing and recording information.
Making a counting or alphabet book	Using alphabetical order. Matching objects to numbers.